SILENT VALLEY AT WAR

Vic Hallam

AS 1942 DREW to a close, Winter arrived with a vengeance in the Derwent Valley. The pale morning sun gave way to cloud, and in the biting cold wind it was snowing. Smoke drifted from stone cottage chimneys as the villagers of Derwent and Ashopton banked up their fires against the cold and settled down to await the New Year.

The scene would have graced a Christmas card, but the festive season that year brought with it little to celebrate. The war with Germany was not going well and loved-ones were away in the armed forces. Food and other essentials were 'on ration', there was a general shortage of goods and little to look forward to.

And there were other, more immediate sources of gloom, for this would be the last Christmas many people would ever spend in the Derwent Valley. Their homes, farms, church and chapels, tree-lined lanes and the beautiful Derwent Valley itself were all to disappear under the new, giant Ladybower Dam, third in a series of dams

Ashopton Viaduct under construction in August 1940, looking north up the Derwent Valley. The old road to Derwent can be seen beside the river, with the *Ashopton Inn* on the right. The present road to Fairholmes is being cut out of the hill on the left.

built to store water in the Upper Derwent Valley, to slake the industrial thirsts of Sheffield, Nottingham, Derby and Leicester. Many villagers remembered the building of Howden and Derwent dams between 1901 and 1916. Since 1935 work had been underway, constructing the huge dam wall at Bamford, erecting concrete viaducts at Ashopton and Ladybower, and finding new paths for the roads that were being diverted around and over the new reservoir.

As the world's powers searched for ways to bring about an end to the conflict, many ideas were put forward. One, by a strange coincidence, also involved dams and the flooding of a valley, but this time it was the destruction of dams and the flooding of a valley in Nazi Germany. Secret tests were already taking place off Chesil Beach near Weymouth, supervised by a scientist named Barnes Wallis, who was developing a spinning spherical mine to be dropped from aircraft, designed to fracture thick concrete walls.

No-one could foresee just how important a part the Derwent Valley would play in that plan over the coming months.

Stone cottages at Derwent, above, in 1940. The 'school' sign warned of the by-then closed village school, although in 1940 Derwent Hall had become an out-station of Sheffield's Notre Dame School for girls (and some younger boys!).

This section of the old road from Bamford to Ladybower, left, can still be seen when the waters are low, just to the Sheffield side of Ladybower viaduct. The buildings are on the (A57) Sheffield road, with the *Ladybower Inn* to the left.

THE OUTBREAK OF war had brought problems for the Derwent Valley Water Board, and for the Scottish firm of Richard Baillie & Sons, contracted to build the Ladybower Dam. Building of the dam had started in 1935, when labour and materials were plentiful, but as war tightened its grip on the British economy, so the supply of both labour and materials became a major problem.

Prices of materials increased weekly; supplies of cement were a constant problem. Holloways, the London firm building the largely concrete Ashopton and Ladybower Viaducts, needed one hundred tons of cement a week and had sixty men employed on site.

At the main site at Yorkshire Bridge, where the immense dam wall was being built, 312 men were working when war broke out. Six months later only 218 remained, such were the demands of war upon the adult male population. And whereas their average wage in September 1939 was around £3. 8s. 10d. (£3.44), by the following March it had increased to around £4.00. In the same period material costs had risen by 12½ percent, and such was the effect this had on the contractors that the Water Board authorised a special additional payment in compensation.

In September 1940 the Vice-Chairman of the Water Board and their engineer, Mr R.W.S. Thompson, attended the Ministry of Health to make direct representations asking for proper supplies of

Looking east across the Derwent Valley in January 1939. The river is already culverted beneath the earthworks for the new dam wall, the line of which is marked by staging and cranes.

LADYBOWER DAM

cement for work on the Reservoir, Viaducts and associated works. Their request was successful, and over the next few months supplies were adequate, although prices still steadily rose.

The price for one hundred tons of Robson's brand of cement from G & T Earle Ltd in September 1940 was £221. 16s. 3d; twenty-five tons of steam coal delivered by the Sheffield firm of E.A. Stevenson cost £29. 3s. 4d. and was enough for six months.

The Water Board was also extrememly worried about the protection of their Howden and Derwent storage reservoirs and other vital areas of their undertaking, all vulnerable to aerial attack, and in January 1939 they undertook to build two air-raid shelters. One was planned at the Yorkshire Bridge Filter Plant close by Ladybower Dam, at a cost of £345, the other at a site on Bamford Filters, costing £360. Work was also carried out to make the Yorkshire Bridge Plant a little less conspicious from the air. Four large tarpaulin sheets costing £8. 15s. each were attached to the roof and skylight area. Also purchased were twenty-four gas masks at 7s. 6d each.

As the war progressed and an understanding grew of just how vulnerable public works were to enemy attack, more steps were taken to

Looking east across Ladybower Dam in November 1943. Already water is impounded to the left of the basic dam wall which is almost finished, though stone facing, towers and overflows have yet to be completed.

Looking north across the completed Ashopton viaduct in April 1943, the month when 617 Squadron did most of their practice flights in this area. Already the waters are backing up the valley, for the valves at Ladybower Dam are shut. Compare this picture with the photo on page one.

safeguard the Derwent Valley Water Board's undertakings, and you will find details of these later in this book.

Once used to the rigours of war, work on the dam and its associated works continued steadily (although it is noteworthy that no work was done between December 1939 and March 1940 due to weather conditions). By 1943 the outlet valves at Ladybower Dam were ready for closing and the impounded waters of the Derwent began steadily to rise.

On 17th March 1943 the last service was held in Derwent Church and most of the village was being demolished. Already the magnificent Hall at Derwent, built in 1672 and added to thereafter, was now almost in ruins. Even this fine building had played its part in the War effort, providing Sheffield's Notre Dame Girls' School with a welcome respite from the bombings that Sheffield had suffered.

The Children's Hospital had also used the Hall as an annexe, and workers on the dam seeking temporary accommodation had been housed there too. Now, in the fading light, its ruins were still majestic.

This was also a very worrying time for Mrs Francis Thorp, who lived at the Derwent Schoolhouse, where she had held the post of caretaker. Now it was her turn to be moved with her three children to a house at Yorkshire Bridge. Archie, her hus-

band, had joined the Royal Artillery early in the War and was now away in Norway, at a time when he was also needed by his family at home.

Mr Thorp had been born at Ronkesley Farm, but had had to move when Howden Dam was built. He had lost two brothers in the Great War. Returning to work with the Water Board after the War, he held the position of General Maintenance Superintendent — a job his son Malcolm would occupy in later years.

During the dry summer of 1989, as the waters of Ladybower subsided, Mrs Thorp was able to stand on the site of her old house at Derwent, and her memories and stories again breathed life into those piles of cherished stone.

So it was then, that despite all the problems, Ladybower Dam was well on its way to being completed by the time the war ended, and the Water Board were making good their plans for a Royal Opening to be held on 25th September 1945. It gave people something to look forward to, and for a time put from their minds the long dark years of war.

Derwent Village School, above, with the schoolhouse behind it, in which lived Mrs Francis Thorp, the school caretaker. Mrs Thorp still returns annually to leave flowers on the Derwent Village memorial, which now stands beside the road overlooking the site of the village.

AS THE PHONEY WAR gave way to a real threat of invasion in May 1940, the Derwent Valley Water Board received a circular from the British Waterworks Association stating that many firms were now forming their own Local Defence Volunteer units, and recommending the Board to do so too; this was agreed. It was also decided that the volunteers would be provided with food whilst on duty. (The Local Defence Volunteers, or LDV, were very soon renamed the Home Guard.)

Also causing grave concern was the method of using unarmed watchmen to protect the reservoirs and works, and the Water Board considered it of the highest importance that the Government should provide an armed military guard for the storage reservoirs and works. The British Water Association was asked to make representations at once to the proper government department, urging them to provide armed protection.

After a series of meetings, the job was given to the Sherwood Foresters, who formed the 15th Battalion. In September 1940 their first assignment was to guard the Water Board's Ambergate Service Reservoir and whilst stationed there they became the 15th (Home Defence) Battalion. About this time the Local Defence Volunteers became the Home Guard. The local unit became the 15th (The Peak) Battalion, Derbyshire, attached to the Sherwood Foresters.

The Water Board Engineer, Mr

Derwent Village had its own cricket team, which played on the open space behind Derwent Hall and beside the river. The photograph below is of the last cricket match before the outbreak of war, whilst the last cricket club dance, above, was held in Derwent School just after the War began.

SILENT VALLEY AT WAR

In the years when our Country was in mortal danger

Frank BINGHAM

who served 10.10.40. - 31.12.44.

gave generously of his time and powers to make himself ready for her defence by force of arms and with his life if need be.

George R.I.

THE HOME GUARD

The certificate issued at the end of the War to Mr Frank Bingham.

R.W.S. Thompson, was asked by the battalion's Officer-in-Charge, Major Ball, if he would accept a post as Captain within the unit, a request aproved by the Water Board. Captain Thompson was awarded a cash grant of two hundred and fifty guineas in recognition of his past services. He, of course, carried on his job as Engineer.

Mr Frank Poynton was at that time employed at Yorkshire Bridge Filters, but wished to take up a full-time appointment in the Home Guard as a paid Sergeant. The Board agreed to his release, holding open his job pending his return at the cessation of hostilities.

Mr Frank Booth, a Water Board employee who lived at Ding Bank Farm, Ashopton — his wife's family home for many years — has fond memories of his early days spent with the LDV and the Home Guard. His unit was based first at Ashopton Chapel, moving to Yorkshire Bridge when the Chapel was demolished to make way for the Ladybower Reservoir.

Mr Booth remembers that, 'Under the Local Defence Volunteers we had no uniforms, just armbands. Weapons were anything we could lay our hands on!'

His first guard duty was high on the Howden Moors at a place known

Mr Frank Booth, left, lived at Ashopton and was in the Home Guard, as well as having a full-time job. Six members of the Bamford platoon on look-out duties on snow-covered Howden Moors, below.

Officers of the 15th Battalion, Derbyshire (The Peak) Home Guard at Coplow Dale in May 1944, with the battalion mascot — a goat — in the centre. Side-arms and batons are in evidence! By 1944 the Home Guard was well equipped, but with little to do, as it was only one month after this photograph was taken that the Allies landed in France on D-Day.

Temporary Nissen huts were put up beside Howden Dam, opposite, for the conscientious objectors who manned the protective smoke screen apparatus.

as 'Fox's Piece', where the unit had a small hut. Along with three others they had one shotgun and four cartridges, and after a night on duty it was work as normal next morning. Mr Booth said there was a bullet hole in the roof of the Vestry at Ashopton Chapel caused by a nervous member of the unit who heard a coughing sound outside which turned out to be a sheep.

Smoke screens surrounded the Dam complex, and these were manned by conscientious objectors who were housed in temporary Nissen huts at Ashopton. Later, a permanent red brick building was erected at a site which is now the Severn Trent Water Board's sawmill, and another building was placed at Howden Dam.

Frank Booth remembers how one night the smoke alarm system was triggered off by a lightning storm, and within minutes the Valley was shrouded in smoke. It affected some of the cows, and at Ding Bank two had to be treated by a vet.

Mr Fred Sutton, whose grandfather Eustace had many years before been a missioner at the workmen's village of Birchinlee during the construction of the Howden Dam (1910-12) and Derwent Dam (1902-16), followed in his father's footsteps by joining the Water Board straight from school. He was later conscripted to work on the Ladybower project, as were many of the Board's employees. Fred also joined the Home Guard unit, attending both Yorkshire Bridge and the Memorial Hall at Bamford. He spent many nights out on the

An early photograph of the Hathersage Home Guard, who appear to have only one rifle between them, although a number of improvised weapons can be seen. The Home Guard was made up of men who were either too young or too old for conscription, or whose jobs exempted them from the call-up.

moors on guard duty and still remembers the welcome breakfast of bacon and eggs served up at Marebottom Cottage by Mrs J. Froggatt, wife of the Howden Dam Keeper .

As petrol was on ration, the Water Board kept a special supply for bursts and other emergencies. To help conserve fuel, they paid 1s. 6d. a week to employees who undertook to deliver messages and so on around the area by push bike. As some of these errands involved as much as a ten-mile round trip, Fred and his colleagues certainly earned their money!

Mr Sutton attended many courses — one was instruction on the Lewis Gun — and six of the Board's employees attended a five-day course at the Sherwood Forester's headquarters at Normanton. Arrangements were also made for Dr Mary Andrews to give instruction to the men on First Aid. There can be little doubt that the dear lady made a first class job of it, and she was a leading light in the ARP who had their unit housed in the Water Board's garages at Bamford.

In later life she became a local legend with her involvement with the Scout movement. I remember only too well attending her home with five others to take our First Aid Badge. After a morning spent digging the back garden, the ones to receive their badges were the ones who came up with the best treatment for back-ache and blisters!

Messrs A.F. Hancock, the local firm of grocers, provided transport for the Home Guard units, as did the Water Board, for which they received 1s per mile. When no transport was available the unit marched to their camp site at Coplow Dale near Tideswell.

A rifle range was set up at Yorkshire Bridge Filters with a .303 range at Edale. Hand grenade practice was held at the Bole Hill Quarry at Grindleford, a site which had been used earlier to obtain stone for the Derwent and Howden Dams. High up in the Derwent Valley an anti-aircraft unit was in place on the towers of the Derwent and Howden Dams and the Home Guard erected barbed wire around the tower bases. The staples which held it in place are still there today.

Strung out across the dams were booms, in the shape of diamonds, to deter sea planes from landing. Major Dickinson, who was in charge of the troops stationed at Midhope, asked for permission to carry out 'opposed landing' training at Howden Dam, a manoeuvre he planned to carry out once a fortnight. The Board agreed, on the understanding that no contamination of the water took place.

Mr Albert Gledall, who now lives at Yorkshire Bridge, moved from Sheffield to Derwent when his father, also named Albert, was appointed caretaker at Derwent Hall, part of which was being used as the unemployed centre.

Albert Junior started working with the Baillees on the dam site, but later moved to Holloways, building Ladybower and Ashopton Viaducts.

About this time, Mr Gledall joined the Home Guard and reported to Ashopton Chapel for his first duty. Albert remembers: 'By the time I joined they were well equipped with uniforms and weapons. I didn't enjoy the drilling and marching much, but the camps at Coplow Dale were good times, as were the trips to the rifle range'.

Mr George Hallam, a local man from Bamford, worked for Richard Baillee between 1936 and 1949 and rose to become a foreman. He joined the Local Defence Volunteers unit at its formation. George remembers much of his time was spent searching for escaped prisoners-of-war, including captured Italians, Germans and Czechs who were put to work at the dam site and Ladybower

Dr Mary Andrews instructed the Home Guard in First Aid. Here she leads the 1st Bamford Scouts in a post-war Remembrance Day Parade at Hope.

Quarry.

The Local Defence Volunteers had little in the way of weapons in those early days, and had no uniform other than armbands. George Hallam, Alf Burton, Frank Watson and a Mr Rose were sent up Win Hill on guard duty, armed only with two wooden brush stakes. Frank also had a mock wooden rifle. After about an hour a dim light was spotted in some trees and as the light drew nearer Frank volunteered to investigate armed with the wooden rifle.

He challenged with the usual, 'Halt, who goes there?' and then added, 'And three others have you covered as well'. Had it been the enemy and not a unit member, he could have been the first to surrender to a brush stake!

Another occasion George remembers well was the 'battle' against the Hathersage unit. The task was to capture Hathersage Railway Station. Two umpires were to judge the event and upon a result would blow a whistle declaring the battle over. All was going well, and part of the Bamford unit approached undetected and were lying in wait close to the station when suddenly a loud whistle was heard.

Thinking it was the signal to end the battle they stood up and then, to their horror, realised it was the station master whistling out the 11.10 am train to Sheffield.

The Home Guard, with mascot, parade through Hathersage, above.

Members of the Timber Corps, left, stripped trees in the Derwent Valley and attempted some arable farming, part of a national attempt to replace imports with home-produced food.

The full Bamford platoon of the Home Guard assembled at the *Marquis of Granby* at Bamford. Behind them is Bamford Station. The white lines painted on the road were designed to assist movement in the wartime blackout.

On Crookhill was a look-out post, as there were on many hilltops in the Peak, from which enemy aircraft could be spotted easily. During the early wartime, when invasion was considered likely and enemy aircraft were bombing towns and cities in the north of England, such posts were important.

One night George Hallam was on duty with his Uncle George Senior (the writer's father!) on Crookhill where there was a dugout and a crows-nest look-out tower. Two other guards were there too, for it was a two-on, two-off watch. George's pal, Harry Heap, famous in Sheffield for his cartoons and sketches of footballers and other personalities in *The Star* , was with them, and when George Senior arrived for his watch he told George Junior to have a look in a large stone close by the dugout. What George saw to his amazement was a full caricature of the Prime Minister at the time, Winston Churchill, complete with cigar, carved in stone. Harry Heap had done it using a hammer and six-inch nails. It still remains there to this day.

Also stationed on Crookhill were the Observer Corps, who had a hut and tower manned throughout the War.

George Hallam Junior was also on duty the night a German aircraft came down on the moors close to Crookhill. Three German airmen were taken prisoner, and as the field telephone was out of action the lads had to go to Crookhill Farm to use Mr S. Elliott's instrument. The officer on duty was housed in the *Derwent Hotel* at Bamford and told them to stay the night at Crookhill until daylight, when the regular army would arrive for the airmen.

The four Home Guards worked out a watch of two-on, two-off and Mr Elliott worked out a rota for his family to watch the local lads and the Germans.

As the war progressed, from 1942

into 1943 and 1944, so the threat of invasion diminished, and was replaced by anticipation of D-Day. But the vigilant Home Guard remained, ready for whatever might befall, until 1945 allowed them to quietly return to something near to a peaceful peacetime life. But as we shall see, the Derwent Valley still had one special task to perform in 1943.

* * * *

Mrs Olive Booth and her husband Frank lived at Ding Bank Farm, Ashopton, Olive's childhood home, which overlooked the site of the Ladybower Dam construction works in the early years of the war. For the time being it had escaped demolition. Frank had been conscripted to work at the cement works at Hope, so he and Olive worked their farm in the evenings.

They clearly remember a night in April 1943 when they were awakened by the deafening roar of low-flying aircraft. Olive jumped from her bed and rushed to the window, convinced the planes were about to crash, but as the distinctive shapes of Lancaster bombers made their way out of the valley, she turned to Frank and said, 'It's just those RAF lads out joy-riding again, wasting petrol. It's a pity when we can't get any for ourselves.' The Lancasters returned to the valley several times more and each time met with the sharp edge of Frank's tongue, for not only was the milk yield down, but the hens at Ding Bank had cut production. Frank believes this was entirely due to the noise of the planes.

Water overflowing Derwent Dam in early wartime, before the Derwent Valley had been overwhelmed by conifers.

It was not long before the Booths found out just what those crews had been doing in the Derwent Valley.

Mrs Marjorie Walker, from nearby Bamford, left her job at Bamford cotton mill for a healthier life with the timber corps, a branch of the Ministry of Supply. The corps was engaged in the felling and stripping of trees for war use and they were active in the Derwent Valley. Marjorie joined other 'locals' from Sheffield, together with teams from Wales and twelve Danish volunteers, who were skilled in the arts of sewing and patching — much sought-after in those days of make-do-and-mend.

One day in March 1943, while working on the western slopes of the valley, Marjorie spotted a lone Lancaster bomber flying very low down the Derwent Valley from north to south. It flewbetween the towers of Derwent Dam at around fifty feet, and as it passed her group the crew of that single plane could be clearly seen. 'For many days that plane was the topic of conversation,' remembered Marjorie recently. 'Then we heard stories of more planes in the valley, and at night in April and early May, so we guessed something was going on. Of course, during May it all became clear to us. The papers told us what they had been doing. We were so proud.'

What Marjorie almost certainly saw was Guy Gibson's first recorded flight down the Derwent Valley on 28th March 1943, after he had been advised that his newly-formed squadron should practice low-flying.

A few days after the successful dams raid in May 1943, Guy Gibson visited Sheffield, promoting the National Savings 'Wings for Victory' week. He stayed the night at Riverdale Grange in Sheffield. In February 1946, Lady Frances Riverdale suggested to the Derwent Valley Water Board that it might be 'possible to name one of the lakes, embankments or roads by his (Gibson's) name . . . as a fitting memorial gesture to one of the most outstanding exploits of the war, and which he led after severe experiments with such splendid skill and daring.'

The Derwent Valley Water Board gave careful and sympathetic consideration to this idea and promised to bear it in mind for the future, but felt there appeared to be no part of the Board's work available at the time which could be appropriately named after Gibson.

And that might have been an end of the matter until in March 1954 the newspapers reported that the Associated British Picture Corporation proposed to film four-engined Lancaster bombers flying low in the vicinity of Derwent Reservoir, as part of a film to be called *The Dam Busters*. The Water Board was rather miffed that this announcement was made before the film company had approached it and accordingly wrote to the Air Ministry pointing out that the land around the dams was owned by the Board. Presumably prompted by the Air Ministry, the film company then wrote to the Board, assuring members that no discourtesy was intended and asking for permission to film in the vicinity of Howden Reservoir. At a meeting on the 29th April 1954, the Board gave its approval.

On Saturday 28th July 1945, the *Sheffield Telegraph* contained an article describing how, whilst the plans for 'dam-busting raids' were being made in this country a system was devised to safe-guard the dams around Sheffield, particularly Strines, Langsett, Underbank and Ewden, often referred to as the Sheffield Lakes. (In those now far-off days, they were owned by Sheffield Corporation, who took a keen interest in their maintenance).

A smoke screen installation was laid down on a scale never before attempted. Devised and carried out by the army, it was possible almost by pressing a button to fill the whole of the Reservoir valleys with a thick smoke through which nothing could be seen. Thirty thousand generation points were built right up in the hills, with some thousands of miles of wire, all needing protection against the winds, rains and snows. Manning the guns and maintaining the smoke installations were five thousand troups bivouacked on the banks of the Reservoirs. The newspaper assured its readers that the Corporation's Water Engineer had made clear to the soldiers the importance of strict hygiene and the dangers of pollution. Rigid inspections had failed to disclose a single instance of breach of the vital orders.

Derwent Hall in the summer of 1940, when it was home to pupils from Sheffield's Notre Dame School. Only the masked headlamp on the car tells of the War.

EVACUATION to DERWENT HALL

IT WAS COMMONLY believed in 1939 that the Declaration of War would be immediately followed by destructive bombing raids, particularly against industrial cities such as Sheffield.

Many of the parents with children at Sheffield's Notre Dame School were keen to see their daughters evacuated.

Although at first Derwent Hall was considered unsuitable for children of school age, a majority of parents decided at a meeting in August 1939 that evacuation should take place, for no other building was available.

Derwent Hall dated back in part to 1672, although it had been added to, most recently with the addition of a private chapel in the late nineteenth-century when the Hall was bought by the Norfolk family. In 1927 the Hall and 120 acres of land had been sold to the Derwent Valley Water Board in anticipation of the building of Ladybower Dam, and since 1932 the Hall had been a Youth Hostel. A large, rather neglected and rambling old stone building, it was plainly not ideal for a boarding school, but in late August 1939, eleven nuns and eight maids went out to clean and prepare Derwent Hall for its new occupants.

On Saturday 1st September the first thirty children arrived, and within days there were 145 scholars in residence, around one-third of Notre Dame's school-roll at the time. The Headmistress later reported on those early days.

'There was not sufficient 'anything', and chairs, tables, china,

This delightful lino-cut, left, was the work of Mr Sanders, Assistant Warden of the Youth Hostel at Derwent Hall. The picture opposite, from an album kindly loaned to us by Notre Dame School in Sheffield, is entitled simply 'Running out to play'.

Around forty years separate the two photographs of the south front of Derwent Hall, with the lower view taken in 1941 shortly before the Hall was demolished. Not only has the ornamental garden been removed, (replaced in part with what looks like a small vegetable plot), but so also have some of the trees behind the Hall. The curious sundial, below, was found at the left end of the wall which separated the Hall from the 'front garden'.

The charming photograph opposite was taken on 29th June, 1940 when, (from left to right starting at the top), John Sawtell, Philippa Darley, Leonie McDonagh, Margaret Westmorland, Peter Granelli and Paul Huntingdon made their First Holy Communion in the chapel at Derwent Hall.

cutlery, everything (except beds) had to be transported from School, in addition to ordinary school equipment, desks, black-boards, pianos *etc*. Parents helped valiantly until petrol shortage began. An immediate need was hot water, and an Ideal Boiler and four bath cubicles had been installed by November, and a hot water supply assured.' She refers also to the 'intense cold' and the 'miserable living quarters'.

As air-raid precautions at the school's Sheffield premises improved, and time was showing that the feared mass-bombing raids were unlikely (and also perhaps, because it seems someone was trying to requisition part of the School's Sheffield buildings!), it was hoped that a return to the City might be made in the Summer of 1940. This was not possible, however, and probably just as well, for two bombs fell in the gardens of the School's Cavendish Street premises during the Sheffield Blitz on 12th Decemeber 1940, shattering almost every window in the school.

Conditions at Derwent Hall rapidly deteriorated in September 1940. 'Domestic service' was inadequate, and 'the place was unbearably dirty, artificial light appalling, the buildings derelict and the fuel stinted'. Not only was life at Derwent Hall unpleasant, but the Headmistress was attempting to manage two schools twelve miles apart, with transport assured to her on only one day each week.

In May 1941, parents were told of the School's decision to withdraw

Outside the chapel — dedicated to St. Henry and added to Derwent Hall by the Norfolk family in the late nineteenth century — sit two Notre Dame scholars. The tranquil scene is reflected idyllically in an ornamental pool.

The west front of Derwent Hall, below, on a 'visitors' day'.

The Terrace, below, flanked the south front of Derwent Hall, with iron gates that led out to the gardens and the chapel, (whose roof can be seen at the end). More signs of wartime cereal production can be seen beyond it.

A late-autumn view of the south front of Derwent Hall and the chapel, above.

Canon Collingwood, left, was Parish Priest at Bamford. He regularly said Mass in the chapel, for pupils and staff and for Catholics from the surrounding area. His liking of snuff is well remembered.

from Derwent Hall in the Summer of 1941. Some campaigned against the return, even appealing to the Board of Education, whose Inspector promptly declared the Hall derelict and living conditions impossible! On 31st July 1941, Notre Dame finally left Derwent Hall.

Looking back on their time at Derwent Hall, the Headmistress wrote thus. 'The older evacuees, 16 to 18-year-olds, found adaptation difficult. They suffered from lack of their reference library, from lack of adequate lighting and heating, from make-shift laboratory accommodation; they felt anxiety for their families left in danger areas, and experienced vague misgivings about the immediate effects of war upon themselves and those dear to them, especially relatives in the Forces. The difficulties incidental to life in a dark, unsuitable building, a life

IN WINTER'S ICY GRIP . . .
The winter of 1940/41 was particularly severe, and snow lay heavy in the Derwent Valley for several weeks. These photographs show the River Derwent, probably just north of the Hall, where woodland skirted the river bank, looking across the river to the Hall, above, and the Pack-horse bridge, right.

crowded with house-cleaning and caring for younger children, with a total lack of the most ordinary comforts, were heroically faced, but took their toll, when the nervous strain of the July examinations was added, and four Higher Schools Certificate candidates failed to obtain the FULL Certificate.

But the remainder of the School, including the 15-year-old School Certificate candidates, fell in love with the life, were insensitive to drawbacks to ordinary educational routine, and gained much from the long walks, freer open-air life, the spice of adventure, and actually achieved 100% Examination successes!

In the following school year, 1940-41, H.S.C. results were excellent. The candidates had adapted themselves to country conditions, though inferior artificial lighting had caused some deterioration of eyesight'.

After reverting for a while to a Youth Hostel, Derwent Hall was finally repossessed by the Water Board in September 1942 and gradually stripped of its valuable bits and pieces. By the Summer of 1943 the Hall was in ruins. But memories endure, and the photographs of Notre Dame's occupation suggest that they are mainly happy ones.

Derwent Church was dedicated to Saints James and John, and was built in 1867. The tower and spire were added in 1873, and here they rise out of a snow-girt landscape, still beckoning the weary traveller to a village that was soon to disappear.

Derwent Post Office, above and right, served a small community and has been replaced by a single collection box which still stands beside the road at Derwent, near the gateposts to the old vicarage.

The stepping stones, right, were one of several such crossings of the Derwent in the vicinity of the Hall and village, for the river below Derwent Dam was at most times gently running.

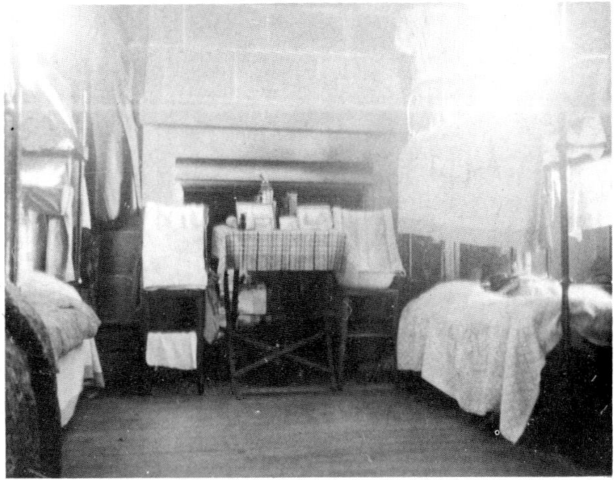

A SCHOOL AT WORK . . . AND PLAY

(Clockwise from the top left corner) Mrs Hallatt was described beneath her photograph as one of the school's devoted helpers. Her Morris 8 car is fitted with a headlamp mask to avoid it being seen by enemy aircraft at night. On Visiting Days parents were brought out from Sheffield by Corporation bus, for petrol was rationed and cars were scarce.

Classrooms, dormitories and even a lab were adapted to fit the existing rooms at Derwent Hall. Dormitory 17 (there were at least nineteen dormitories!) shows strong signs of YHA influence, for Derwent Hall had been a Youth Hostel for several years. The First Form classroom, below, looks to have been in what was once the ground floor Drawing Room, which was richly panelled with oak, which probably matched the desks and easels! The group of five girls hold up their identity cards and the labels given to all evacuees. One also carries a gas mask over her shoulder, which was supposed to be carried at all times.

Form II

Form III

Form IV

House Captains

Form V

n VI

AH! QU'IL EST BON LE BON DIEU

EVACUATION SCRAP-BOOK

NOTRE DAME at DERWENT HALL

1940-1941

Bridge End Farm was also known as Shepherd's Farm — the name of the family who lived there for many years. It stood on the west side of the river, across from Derwent Hall. Linking the two was an ancient stone Pack-horse bridge, older even than the Hall, which was removed and rebuilt at Slippery Stones at the head of Howden Dam.

The view across the meadow to the back of Bridge End Farm, below, was taken from just below the present road at Bridge End car park.

THE DAMBUSTERS

OVER THE YEARS since the end of the Second World War, stories have developed from the memories of people and their brave deeds in those dark days. Details slowly develop and an impression is created which can become in time more legendary than historical.

Operation Chastise has become one such legend, the story of that epic night of 16th-17th May in 1943, when a group of very brave flyers dropped their bombs on German dams and wrote themselves into the annals of history; a night when they became *The Dambusters*.

Even though the Royal Air Force came formally into being in 1918, it was not until 1936 that separate Commands were created for fighters and bombers. At the outbreak of the War, RAF Bomber Command could hardly have been described as well-equipped, having only thirty-three squadrons of twin-engined aircraft. Early air attacks seemed fairly ineffective, and often involved nothing more offensive than leaflets.

But from 1940, and later with the introduction of the four-engined Halifax, Stirling and Lancaster, the strategic bombing of Germany really began. The aim was the progressive destruction and dislocation of the enemy military, industrial and economic systems to the point where his capacity for resistance would be fatally weakened.

One man who was totally committed to the war effort was a quiet, unassuming civilian aircraft designer who, when hostilities com-

Wing Commander Guy Gibson, who led 617 Squadron on the dams raid.

As early as 1937 the Air Ministry identified the ideal of destroying the Möhne and Sorpe dams. Barnes Wallis was assistant chief designer at Vickers Armstrong's aviation section in 1939 and it was his doggedness and undoubted genius that developed the unique 'bouncing bomb' — in fact, a depth charge — used by 617 Squadron.

menced, was determined to make his own personal contribution towards shortening the War and ensuring victory. His name was Barnes Wallis and, at fifty-three, he had been designing for Vickers-Armstrong since before the First World War. He had designed the Wellesley, an aircraft which captured the world's non-stop record and, later, the Wellington bomber which proved to be the mainstay of Bomber Command during the first three years of the War.

Many targets for bombardment had been selected, mainly basic sources of power, such as coal-mines, oil dumps and power stations. But foremost in Barnes Wallis' mind were the great dams supplying the industrial Ruhr.

Barnes Wallis was well aware that existing aircraft and weapons were of little use to carry out an attack on such a target with any hope of success, so he set out to rectify the situation, and after a great deal of research he came up with an acceptable answer — a ten-ton bomb carried by a fifty-ton bomber operating at a height of 40,000 feet.

The bomb would exceed the speed of sound as it fell, burying itself deep in the earth and exploding to create a minor earthquake with considerable destructive power.

After all the research, the idea was looked upon with scepticism by the powers-that-were, perhaps understandably so. Was this the right time to risk diverting any part of the war effort on a wild experiment that might prove fruitless?

But Barnes Wallis continued to experiment and found that a five-ton bomb, a load which the new four-engined Lancaster bomber was capable of carrying, could breach a dam the size of the Möhne providing the bomb could be placed to explode *alongside* the dam wall and *below* the surface of the water. A torpedo-type bomb was of no use as the Germans had anti-torpedo nets strung across the dam below water level.

This led to the concept of a 'bouncing' bomb or mine, which would skip across the surface of a reservoir. Further research and model testing proved it feasible.

Armed with his theories, Barnes Wallis set out to convince the powers-that-were that he really could place a bomb in the right area and breach the dams. The go-ahead was given, and on 4 December 1942 a converted Wellington bomber took off, carrying the first bouncing bomb. Matt Summers was the pilot, and Barnes Wallis acted as bomb aimer. Speed and height mattered little at this stage — something around 200 feet and 200 mph would do. The main test was to see if two tons of spinning metal would act according to plan.

Considerable vibration could be felt throughout the aircraft from the motor which span the mine up to speed before it was dropped. As Matt Summers drew level, Barnes Wallis pressed the button to release the bomb and, spinning backwards, it fell from the aircraft, crashing into the sea and sank in a white mass of spray. Suddenly it reappeared, lurching upwards and then fell back into the murky waters — something was drastically wrong. It was later found that the mine casing had cracked.

After several journeys to Sheffield to discuss the problems with steel experts, tests were resumed, until after several more test-drops with strengthened casings on the mine and even wooden spheres, Barnes Wallis' theory was proved. The correct combination of height, speed and spinning speed of the mine was established. On Sunday 23 January a wooden sphere released from a Wellington bounced twenty or more times! Barnes Wallis' idea worked!

The race was now on, as the time to breach the dams would be in May 1943 when they were full.

To carry out the mission it was decided to form a special squadron. The man chosen to command it was Wing Commander Guy Gibson who, at the age of twenty-five, had already been awarded the DSO and DFC and bar. He had distinguished himself on both fighter and bomber squadrons and, whilst with Fighter Command, had spent many nights defending the skies over Sheffield, even during the Blitz of December 1940.

The special squadron was formed at RAF Scampton in Lincolnshire on 16 March 1943, becoming 617 squadron. The aircrews chosen were hand-picked from the units of No 5 Group, Bomber Command and they really were the 'cream'. Not only did they come from every corner of the British Isles but also from America, Canada, New Zealand and Australia.

On a visit to Derwent Dam in 1986, Squadron Leader Dave Shannon — who took part in the fateful raid — recalled those early days of 617 Squadron's formation.

Flight Lieutenant (later Squadron Leader) Dave Shannon and his crew in 617 Squadron.

'The Squadron, known only as 'X' until given the number 617 some time later, commenced forming up on 16th March 1943.

Within the first few days we got ourselves pretty well organised, with about ten conventional Lancasters which had been borrowed from other squadrons.

Guy Gibson called all the crews together to give us a rundown on the training we were to undertake — low level formation flying, pinpoint navigation and low-level bombing by day and by moonlight. We had to achieve perfection at 150 feet. Cross-country perfection was planned, with navigation by map reading and dead reckoning over the sea. No inkling was given as to the target we were to attack and security was as tight as a drum.

Our training began with low-level flying by daylight — first singly and then in formations of three aircraft. I think most of us had been on several low-level daylight raids with our previous squadrons. This was different though, as 150 feet was considerably lower than we had been permitted to fly before. To begin with we mapped out our own routes, but this created immediate havoc with the powers-that-be, as complaints of low-level Lancasters were coming in from all parts of the country.

Cross-country was stopped for a couple of days, then we were given three or four set routes, planned to avoid the trouble spots. To counteract the shortage of moonlight we practiced at dawn and dusk, but even so, we needed more realistic moonlight conditions.

This was achieved by lining the

The early training runs of 617 Squadron Lancasters are commemorated in this fine pencil drawing by Mike Murphy, above. Most training runs followed a north to south route over Bradfield and the dams at Damflask and Agden, and across to Howden and Derwent. This gave low-flying practice through the valleys and a final low-level run over the Derwent Dam.

Guy Gibson's log book for April 1943, right, includes references to Derwent and the 'Sheffield lakes' and the extensive cross-country training undertaken.

Month	Date	Type	No.	1st Pilot	or Passenger	Results and Remarks
—	—	—	—	—	—	— Totals Brought Forward
APRIL	1	LANCASTER	3	SELF	CREW	LOCAL.
						CREW. P/O TEAROIT.
						P/O SPAFFORD
						F/LT TREVOR-ROPER
						F/LT HUTCHISON
						P/O DEERING
						SGT PULFORD.
"	4	"	B	"	"	TO LAKE NR SHEFFIELD
"	5	"	D	"	"	SCOTTISH X COUNTRY. LAKES.
"	9	"	D	"	"	BASE-DERWENT RESERVOIR
"	11	MAGGIE	–	"		- UPPINGHAM RES. - BASE.
				SELF	F/LT MAY.	LOCAL MANSTON.
						CRASHED IN FIELD. OK.
"	15	OXFORD	–	SELF	TWO CREW	BASE- READING. FAIROAKS-BASE
"	15	MOSQUITO	4098	S/L LONGBOTTOM (SHORTY)	SELF	FAIROAKS - WEYBRIDGE-
"	16	LANCASTER	Y	SELF	CREW	CORNISH X COUNTRY AT
						LOW LEVEL WITH DUMMY
						ATTACKS ON LAKES
"	20	LANCASTER	J	SELF	FAY + CREW	NIGHT X COUNTRY TO
						MANY RESERVOIRS WITH
						DUMMY ATTACKS

Lancaster cockpits with blue perspex and the crews wearing yellow-tinted goggles. The effect was very eerie — one had a strong desire to tear the goggles off and see what the hell was happening, but on overcoming that urge one realised it offered a pretty fair comparison with moonlight flying and was certainly better than dawn and dusk flying. I suppose that by the end of April Gibson knew the targets and the type of weapon to be used.

During that period secret experiments were being carried out dropping the mines. These took place at Reculver near Margate. It had been found that by dropping them at the speed of 240 mph from 150 feet the outer case shattered, so Barnes Wallis had to go back to square one. The eventual solution showed a successful operation would mean flying at 220 mph and releasing the bare cylinder mines at 60 feet on the run-in.

So it was late in our training when the height for flying was lowered from 150 feet to 60 feet, and flying at 60 feet in daylight is very different to flying at 60 feet at night! The only way we could fly at that level without killing ourselves would require a very accurate altimeter, but no such thing existed in those days.

Once again the research experts were asked for ideas. The problem was overcome by putting one spotlight on the nose of the aircraft and one on the tail, with the angle of the beams set to converge into one spot at exactly 60 feet below the aircraft. Having flown around the country at

150 feet we then had to start again flying lower. This, along with the low-level formation flying and accurate bombing runs at 60 feet, were major problems to resolve and this is where our practice over the Derwent Dam started in earnest.

The spotlight system worked well. A lot of practice was done over Scampton and then we moved on to flying over water, and for this the Derwent Dam was very much favoured.

The problem was getting down from 150 feet to the perfect spot of light at 60 feet. This was done by the navigator looking through the side blister in the cockpit and calling to the pilot through the intercom — 'Down, down, down, down' — until the spots converged, making one spot on the water.

It proved very successful but fairly dicey. At first one thought the chap calling 'Down, down' would never stop.

A week or so before the raid we saw what later proved to be the mines coming in by road transport on low-loaders, and being taken straight to the bomb dump. We didn't see them again until 16th May, when they were brought out for loading.

Another gadget to help the bomb-aimer was the penny bomb sight. This 'V' notch sight had two pointers which, when lined up with the towers on the Dam, gave the correct distance to release the mine from the wall. So again it was back to Derwent for more practice.

To achieve the required bouncing of the mine itself, it was necessary to impart reverse spin to it. This was done by a variable-speed hydraulic motor belt-driven system which created very bad vibration throughout the plane.

When released, the mine behaved rather like a flat stone thrown and skipping across the water. The mine, 'Upkeep' as it was known, looked like the front end of a steam roller. It was designed to be carried athwartships and rotated about an axle through its centre. Two caliper suspension arms from the bomb bay clamped onto the axle on each side.

When the bomb-aimer pressed his bomb release button these arms sprang apart, thus allowing it to drop straight down, and as it was already revolving it would bounce across the water. The aircraft speed gave it momentum which, combined with the reverse spin, made sure it didn't bury itself in the water.

Barnes Wallis' 'bouncing bomb' was actually a mine or depth charge, code-named 'Upkeep'. Frequently likened to the front wheel of a steam-roller, the mine weighed 9250 lbs including 6000 lbs of underwater explosive. Six feet long and 50 inches in diameter, the mine was fitted with detonators designed to go off at a depth of 30 feet.

The Eder Dam on 17th May 1943.

On 15 May, Guy Gibson called his pilots to the Briefing Room at Scampton and told us what our targets were. Many were relieved, for they had thought it was to be the German battleship, Tirpitz, *or U-boat pens. He also said that if the weather held the raid was to go ahead the following night.*

On the morning of 16 May the weather reports were good, so the green light was given. Reconnaissance had shown that the dams were full, perfect for the raid. One sadness was that Guy's pet black Labrador, Nigger, was run over outside the gates at Scampton on the day of the raid, and was instantly killed. Guy asked that Nigger be buried at midnight, the time that Guy would be over the Möhne Dam. His wish was fulfilled.

Many years later, when some members of the original Squadron met at Woodall Spa — where there is a 617 Squadron memorial — for a re-union, they were sitting for a group photo when suddenly a black Labrador appeared from nowhere, sat with us for the photo-session, after which it promptly left. A local newspaper ran an ad to see if anyone knew who the dog belonged to, but to this day no-one knows either the dog or its owners.

Nineteen Lancs took off on that epic night of 16th/17 May 1943, and only eleven returned. Fifty-three men perished and three became prisoners-of-war. Mick Martin, one of the RAFs finest pilots, said later that he had problems at sixty feet with insects hitting the Lanc's cockpit screen. He couldn't tell which were insects and which were hazards outside the aircraft, such as poles and power lines and so on.

Mick found a way round this problem by moving his head from side to side to identify the dead insects, which stayed still! Mickie said there were also problems over the dam, as each mine sent up a plume of white water hundreds of feet into the air. As the next Lanc started its run, it was as if the whole area was shrouded in a wet mist.

This was on top of all the other problems we had to contend with!

When the Möhne dam wall broke, Micky Martin was making a cross run to draw fire from the next attacking aircraft. He said later, that as the wall gave way, a large tongue of water hurled from the rupture. Soon the whole valley was flooded, although flames still erupted from the wrecked power station just below the dam wall.

I was in the second flight that night, and had just been called by Guy Gibson to prepare to attack the Möhne dam when we realised that the fourth mine — Young's — had actually breached it, although Maltby did drop a fifth, for no-one was quite sure until we could see the breach with our own eyes. It was a fabulous sight.

The three of us left with bombs at the Möhne then moved on with Gibson and Young to our next target, the Eder dam, set deep down in vallies and by now already shrouded in fog. It was harder to bomb than the Möhne, because the outlet was steeper and the hills so close to the Lanc's pull-out point. But as the Eder was the largest dam in Germany, it was the prize needed most to guarantee the raid's success!

I went in first, and after several dummy runs dropped my mine. We thought we'd done it, there was a great spout of water, but no apparent breach. It was Les Knight's bomb that brought that about, after Maudsley had tried.

Bill Townsend, who was leader of Wave Three, arrived home at Scampton the following day in daylight, after much time spent in searching for the third target, the Ennepe Dam. Bill made a direct-hit on the wall, causing damage but no breach. His crew were full of praise for his flying skills. At one stage they said he flew his Lancaster through a clearing in the forest at a height of only twenty-five feet, with only three feet clearance on his wingspan, to avoid German guns that would almost certainly have brought them down.

Bill makes light of this today, typical of this super gentleman. Those of us that came back — and the loss of life that night was tragic — we all had a tale to tell.❜

The Möhne Dam on the day after the raid, with water still gushing through the hundred-metre-wide breach. The pipework in the foreground is all that remained of the power station.

Another view of the Möhne Dam after the Dambusters had left their calling cards. The similarity with Derwent Dam is plain.

So what did the Dams Raid achieve? On the credit side the Möhne Dam was breached and 134 million tons of water poured out to starve the Ruhr of the domestic and industrial needs of a very vital community. The Eder Dam was also breached. This is the largest dam in Germany, and on that night lost some 202 million tons of water, creating havoc in its path. The top of the Sorpe Dam earth retaining wall was also damaged.

On the debit side were the tremendously heavy losses of aircrew and aircraft. Of those who attacked the Möhne and Eder Dams, only five crews returned — those of Gibson, Martin, Maltby, Shannon and Knight.

The men lost were Hopgood, shot down over the Möhne Dam; Young, shot down on the return flight; Maudsley, lost after his bomb overshot the Eder Dam; Astell, shot down on the way in.

From the five aircraft of Wave 2 tasked with attacking Sorpe Dam, McCarthy was the only aircraft to fulfill an attack. Monro was damaged by flak over the Dutch coast on the way in and had to return early; Rice hit the sea on the trip in and ripped his bomb off, so he also returned early. Barlow was hit by flak over the Dutch coast and was also lost on the way in. Byers met with flak over the coast and was lost on the way in.

A reserve wave of five Lancasters took off later that night, to provide back-up or secondary target attacks. Ottley was to attack Lister Dam but was shot down before he could attack. Townsend, after much searching in very bad fog, made a direct hit on the Ennerpe Dam; Brown was assigned to the Sorpe Dam; Burpee was shot down over the Dutch coast and Anderson was diverted by flak and returned late with his bomb intact.

The final total for that fateful night was eight aircraft missing, with 53 men lost, of whom three were taken prisoner. But this spectacularly effective operation earned the Squadron thirty-three decorations, including the Victoria Cross for Guy Gibson, and the Squadron passed gloriously into legend and history as *The Dambusters*.

A ROYAL VISIT

DESPITE all the problems caused by the War, Ladybower Dam was well on its way to completion by the time the armistice had been signed. The outlet valves had been closed and the impounded waters were rising slowly. Arrangements were being made for an Inauguration Ceremony to be held in the Autumn of 1945.

Sir Albert Atkey, the Water Board Chairman, had already had an interview with Sir Alan Lascelles, the King's Private Secretary at Buckingham Palace, where he had been informed that His Majesty had graciously consented to open the Dam. They also discussed the guest list and the format of the ceremony.

At a board meeting on 17th August 1945 held in Nottingham,

Planting the King's Oak at the head of Howden Dam, above left. Throughout the visit, King George VI was accompanied by Queen Elizabeth, now the Queen Mother. The most lasting memorial to that day — 25th September 1945 — are the commemorative tablets unveiled by the King, shown on the previous page. They still stand beside the main road at Ladybower Dam.

On her arrival at the dam, above right, Her Majesty was presented with a bouquet by Sheena Baillee, grand-daughter of the contractor who built the dam.

Sir Albert stated that he had received official confirmation from the King's Secretary that His Majesty would be accompanied by the Queen (our present Queen Mother!) to perform the opening ceremony on Tuesday, 25th September next. Long discussions took place as to the guest list and it was agreed to construct an enclosure capable of accommodating six hundred people, and also that each board member be given six tickets for their own use.

Spaces were also reserved for the children of Bamford Council School.

One of its pupils on that historic day was Mr John Ollerenshaw, who remembers well the 'treat' of being allowed to witness the royal visit, even if it did mean a two-mile round walk to attend the event. 'We were given a small Union Flag to wave, but the memory that remained with me longest was the congestion after the visit, caused by people trying to make their way home and cars blocking the roads for miles — something never seen before in Bamford.'

On 26th August the members of the Board held a full dress rehearsal, with the Chairman playing the role of the King. All was reported to have gone very well, although no-one had taken into account the 55,000 'extras' who would turn up for the real event. It was also agreed to ask the King to plant an oak tree at the head of Howden Dam and to place a box or casket beneath one of the stones on the east overflow crest at Ladybower.

The day started with the arrival of the Royal Train at Victoria Station, Sheffield, where the Lord Mayor and other local officials greeted the royal party. The Queen wore a beige dress and matching hat, whilst the King wore the uniform of Admiral of the Fleet. After a small reception, the royal couple were driven through the streets of Sheffield at five miles-an-hour so that as many people as possible could see them. When the outskirts of the city were reached normal speed was resumed. Derbyshire police had asked people to keep their cars away from the Ladybower area, and many people journeyed by foot from Sheffield and surrounding districts.

After a tour of the Upper Derwent Valley, where the King planted his oak tree, the royal couple arrived at Ladybower at 4 pm, where Miss Sheena Baillie, the grand-daughter of the Contractor, presented Her Majesty with a bouquet of pink carnations.

The royal party then moved on to the east roadside to unveil the Memorial Tablets, after which Sir Albert Atkey handed the King the key to the main gates of Ladybower for him to perform the opening ceremony.

At Ladybower the overflow water is released down two funnel- shaped shafts, each eighty feet in diameter, and the next duty for the King was to lay a stone on the east overflow crest after a copper cylinder had been placed beneath it. This contained coins of the period, a copy of *The Times* newspaper, and a brochure describing the water undertaking.

Tea followed in the Water Board's Filter House where a very special Royal loo had been installed and guarded very closely. Alas, it was not called upon and spent a redundant day with not so much as a 'Royal Flush'. After the usual goodbyes and thank yous, Their Majesties rejoined the Royal Train at Bamford for the journey back to London.

At a subsequent board meeting the Chairman stated he had received a letter from the King's Secretary which read as follows:—

My Dear Sir Albert

The King and Queen were greatly impressed by the Ladybower Reservoir, and much appreciated the very warm welcome given them.

The King desires me to congratulate you and the Members of the Board on the excellence of the arrangements made for the inauguration ceremony.

Everything went extremely well and Their Majesties much enjoyed the day.

The Clerk later read other letters of congratulations from Townships and City dignatories. He also subjected a list of persons and firms to whom acknowledgements were due for assistance given in connection with the royal visit.

The list included The Mayor of Derby for decorations and Mr TS Wells, Parks Supervisor in Derby, for floral decorations. Rolls Royce and Sir Arthur Sidgreaves had loaned the car and chauffeur for the King and Queen and the LNER and Mr HS Thompson and Mr Eugene of Royal Victoria Hotel, Sheffield were acknowledged for their catering.

Also mentioned were Crown Derby Ltd, Derby Works, for the loan of a tea set; The St John's Ambulance services; the Town Clerk of Sheffield and Mr Syratt for arrangements and the reception in Sheffield. Mr T Pratt, an antique dealer from Derby, had loaned silver vases; the Sherwood Foresters' Band had provided music; Mudford's Marquees lent furniture, whilst Water Board staff were thanked for erecting fencing and various other jobs, including keeping the marquees

King George VI placed a copper cylinder containing coins and a newspaper beneath a stone on the east overflow crest on the Ladybower Dam. Behind the chairman of the Water Board stands a young stonemason, Mr Jimmy Reid, who still treasures the (now silver-plated) hammer he handed the King to lay the stone that day.

standing during gales.

The Board also agreed to pay a bonus of £100, split between sixty of its workmen who worked on the Royal Visit.

The day was described later as a highlight in Peak history, and gave many people something to enjoy, and for a time, put from their minds the long dark days of war.

As life in the area slowly returned to something like normal, it was a time to rebuild for the people of Ashopton and Derwent, most of whom by now lived at Yorkshire Bridge or in nearby villages. It meant a completely new way of life for men returning from the forces and those in the Home Guard. The friendships formed would remain with them throughout their lives, standing them in good stead for the years that followed, for the survivors of those dark war years are still the warmest and most genuine people you could meet.

The King's last task was to formally open the valves, above, to release water from the dam into the River Derwent, right. In the distance and to the left can be seen the houses built in 1938 at Yorkshire Bridge by the Derwent Valley Water Board, to rehouse people who had given up their homes to industrial Britain's insatiable demand for water.

AT THE END OF THE DAY

MANY YEARS HAVE passed since those Lancasters of 617 Squadron flew down the Derwent Valley on their training runs. A lot of water has passed under the viaduct at Ashopton, beneath which lie still the village ruins. Never again will the bells of Derwent Church ring out in the Valley, and those dark days of war are long gone.

The chatter of visitors, the bleeting of sheep high on the moors, and the moan of the wind as it threads its way through the pine trees around the dams, these are the gentle sounds of the valley today. The peace is now rarely disturbed, but there have been visits — in 1954 to make the famous film — and since then several times by the same Lancaster of the RAFs Battle of Britain Memorial Flight as it pays tribute to the brave men who gave their lives on the famous Dambusters' raid.

One such occasion was in 1986, on 2nd October at 3.15 in the afternoon when for a few moments time stood still and, for a group of very special men, memories came flooding back. The Dambusters had returned to the Derwent Valley.

The occasion was the unveiling ceremony of a permanent memorial to 617 Squadron. Placed in the entrance of the West Tower of Derwent Dam it meant, for me, the end of a project that had begun a year before.

One late-summer Sunday in 1985 I was approached at Derwent Dam by a smart-looking gentleman who asked if it would be possible to have a quick look around the West Tower. As we strolled along the walkway we talked of the Valley and how the Derwent Dam had been used to train The Dambusters. It was then that the gentleman said he had been a member of the squadron — his name was Mr George Powell. I later found out that 'Chiefy' Powell had been Guy Gibson's right-hand man and was much-loved by the whole squadron.

The Derwent Memorial, installed in the West Tower of Derwent Dam and unveiled on 2nd October 1986.

Mr Powell said he was surprised and saddened that no permanent memorial had been erected to the Squadron in the Valley, considering the important part it had played in the raid. Before he left I made him a promise that something would be done to rectify this. So, over the winter months I decided to attempt to raise money for a memorial stone by staging an exhibition in the West Tower of Derwent Dam. No entrance fee was charged but donations were asked for.

First the permission of Severn Trent Water Authority was required to place a memorial stone on the Dam and to use the West Tower as an exhibition centre. As the dam is still very much in use, I had my doubts, but the reply I received from the Severn Trent management team was excellent. Permission was given to proceed, with help if needed — a magnificent gesture.

The next problem was the purchase and carving of the Memorial Stone, but just one visit to Messrs. E Parrimore & Sons works in Sheffield solved this for me. Mr Parrimore chose to use a special piece of York sand-stone he had been keeping for years, the sort of stone you could spend a life-time searching quarries for, and this was just the memorial it had been waiting for!

The end result was superb. While the stone was being carved, Radio Sheffield broadcast from the works and interviewed Mr Parrimore and his two sons.

In my search for items for the exhibition I contacted the present 617 Squadron which is based at Marham in Norfolk. The officer commanding at that time was Wing Commander Peter Day, who had once been with the *Red Arrows*. Peter not only supplied me with just about all I needed from the Squadron archives, but said he would attend the unveiling ceremony and provide a fly-past of his present day Tornado jet aircraft.

We also had on show one of the finest collections of model aircraft to be seen anywhere, hand-made by local man Brian Potts. This was a marvellous asset to the exhibition.

I had allowed myself just six weekends to raise the necessary money. People attended in their hundreds and not only was enough money raised for the Derwent Memorial, but a cheque was given to Dave Shannon for the Woodall Spa Memorial. This was in memory of the airmen of 617 Squadron who died from 1943 to 1945.

Good news arrived from the Ministry of Defence on 8th September. It was agreed to allow the last remaining Lancaster to fly over the dams on the day the memorial was unveiled, which was fixed for 2nd October.

Everything had gone very well so far, and all we needed now was a fine day. During the first part of the week the valley was shrouded in mist but 2nd October turned out to be like a summer's day.

The day started with Dave Shannon being interviewed on Radio Sheffield. Radio Sheffield had been a marvellous help to us, and later that day came also to the unveiling.

But before the ceremony, a lunch was held at the *Angler's Rest* in nearby Bamford, attended by officials from Severn Trent Water, and past and present members of 617 Squadron. After lunch the party left for Derwent Dam, which by now was surrounded by thousands of people. (The police estimated about 24,000 people).

Dave Shannon, a former Flight Commander of the 617 Squadron and present Chairman of the Squadron Association then unveiled the memorial stone. He spoke about the raid and of his memories of the valley. Then came a hum of excitement as the crowds waited for the fly-past. The Lancaster came first and was a truly spectacular sight, flying down the valley and between the towers. Seconds later, four jet-engined Tornadoes from 617 Squadron roared overhead. It was was an intensely moving experience, and a quiet descended on the valley, as each person thought his or her own thoughts. There weren't many dry eyes in the Derwent Valley that afternoon.

It remains only to remember those remarkable men who, one night in 1943 flew out to create a legend. The debt we owe them can never be repaid, but together we can see that it is not forgotten. To that end there stands now a memorial to them in the Silent Valley.

So be it.

Forty-three years before unveiling the Derwent Memorial, above, Squadron Leader Dave Shannon was photographed, left. with Guy Gibson (in flying jacket). Born in Australia, Dave Shannon joined the RAAF in 1940 at the age of eighteen. He was soon awarded his pilot's badge and arrived in England via the USA and Canada. He flew with Gibson's 106 Squadron at Coningsby and joined 617 when it was formed for the dams raid.

The Battle of Britain Memorial Flight Lancaster — the last Lancaster in Britain — overflew Derwent Dam in 1988, forty-fifth anniversary of the famous dams raid.

Author's Acknowledgements . . .

SO MANY PEOPLE have helped with information, photographs and ideas, and I thank them all. If I have forgotten anyone, I apologise. But I must give particular thanks to the following people for the kind help and support they have given me.

First, to my wife, Robinetta, and daughters, Vicky, Linsey and Fiona; I could not have made it without you! Also to Mr L Feather, who painted the special cover picture; Mr RD Porter; Mr ML Murphy; Mr R Bunting; Mr J Ollerenshaw; Mr R Froggatt; Mr R Robinson; Mr S Yates; Mr M Thorp; Mr B Hazlehurst; Mr D Keaton; Mr E Hawthorne; 617 Squadron, RAF Marham; 617 Sqdn Assn; Squadron Leader D Shannon DSO & Bar, DFC & Bar; Flight Lieutenant B Townsend DFM, CGM; Flight Lieutenant 'Chan' Chandler DFC & Bar, Russian Medal of Valor; Mr JW Kenton; Derrick Warren, Peter Bacon and Mr PM Booth for photos; Mrs F Thorp; Mr & Mrs F Booth; Mr J Elliott; Mr & Mrs F Sutton; Mr & Mrs A Firth; Mr A Gledall; Mr G Hallam; Mrs Bingham; Mrs JS Frost and Sister Ellen of Notre Dame School. And to the Ministry of Defence, Severn Trent Water, the Imperial War Museum, Sheffield Newspapers and the Local History Library in Sheffield.

. . . and dedication

This book is dedicated to all those good people who helped to make possible a permanent memorial at Derwent Dam to the Dambusters.